MOTORCYCLE ROAD RACING

MotoR Mania

by Jeffrey Zuehlke

Jeffrey San George, consultant

Lerner Publications Company • Minneapolis

Special thanks to Darwin Holmstrom and James Michels, retired motorcycle road racers

For Graham—fastest kid on two wheels
For Gus—louder than a 990cc engine at full throttle

Cover Photo: Racers round a turn during the German Moto Grand Prix in Chemnitz.

Lerner Publications Company
A division of Lerner Publishing Group, Inc.
241 First Avenue North
Minneapolis, MN 55401 U.S.A.

Website address: www.lernerbooks.com

Library of Congress Cataloging-in-Publication Data

Zuehlke, Jeffrey, 1968–
    Motorcycle road racing / by Jeffrey Zuehlke.
        p. cm. — (Motor mania)
    Includes bibliographical references and index.
    ISBN 978–0–8225–9427–7 (lib. bdg. : alk. paper)
    1. Motorcycle racing—Juvenile literature. I. Title.
    GV1060.Z84 2009
    796.7′5—dc22   2008025630

Manufactured in the United States of America
1 2 3 4 5 6 – DP – 14 13 12 11 10 09

Contents

Introduction
What Is Motorcycle Road Racing?   4

Chapter One
Motorcycle Road Racing History   6

Chapter Two
Motorcycle Road Racing Culture   22

Motorcycle Road Racing Gallery   34

Glossary   46

Selected Bibliography   46

Further Reading   46

Websites   46

Index   47

What would it feel like to ride a motorcycle at 200 miles (320 kilometers) per hour? How would it feel to slide your knee on the track as you lean your bike into a turn at 120 miles (193 km) per hour? Motorcycle road racers push their bikes to the limit in every race. And they do it without a car or cockpit to protect them. Mistakes can be brutal. What would it feel like to get thrown off a motorcycle at 150 miles (241 km) per hour?

Motorcycle road racing is an exciting and dangerous sport. Years ago, riders competed on road courses—public roads that had been closed off for racing. For safety reasons, most modern events take place on tracks made just for racing. Each asphalt-paved track has its own unique layout. But they all feature tight turns, slow bends, and long straights that test the riders' skill and courage.

With all its action and drama, motorcycle road racing is one of the world's most popular sports. Races are held on five continents. Riders from across the globe compete in many different series. The top level of racing is the MotoGP World Championship. MotoGP (short for motorcycle grand prix) features the world's top riders on the world's most advanced racing bikes. Every professional rider dreams of winning the MotoGP World Championship. But only a few have earned the right to be called the best of the best.

Riders race into the first turn at the 2008 Spanish Grand Prix.

Chapter One

MOTORCYCLE ROAD RACING HISTORY

The motorcycle combines two important inventions of the late 1800s—the bicycle and the gasoline-powered internal combustion engine.

The Hildebrand and Wolfmuller was the first motorcycle to be built and sold for purchase. Introduced in 1894, the German-built machine had a top speed of 25 miles (40 km) per hour.

In fact, early motorcycles weren't much more than bicycles with motors attached to the frame.

Those early bikes weren't very fast. But that didn't stop their riders from doing what came naturally—racing. By the early 1900s, racing was popular in both Europe and the United States. Most European races took place on public roads that had been closed off for the event. Races in the United States usually took place on dirt tracks that were normally used for horse racing.

In time, the races became more organized. In the United States, a group of motorcyclists created the Federation of American Motorcyclists (FAM). The following year, several European motorcycling clubs formed the Federation of International Motorcycle Clubs (FICM).

The FAM and FICM organized races. They created rules for competition and safety. For example, riders had to earn licenses to prove they had the skills to race in official events.

Championship Series

The FAM soon went out of business. So in 1924, riders formed the American Motorcycle Association (or AMA, which later became the American Motorcyclist Association) to take its

7

place. The AMA went on to create the Grand National, the country's first series of national championship races. Riders battled it out on dirt tracks, on tracks made out of wood boards, and on muddy or dusty roads.

Meanwhile, Europeans focused on road racing. The most important races of the season were called grand prix (GP), French for "grand prize." Events at the Isle of Man and in the Netherlands were called Tourist Trophies (TTs).

Riders set out for a race in 1925 on Germany's AVUS (Automobil Verkehrs und Übungs Strasse).

The Isle of Man TT

The Isle of Man is a small island located in the middle of the Irish Sea, off the coast of Great Britain. For 50 weeks a year, the island is the quiet home to about 80,000 people. But for two weeks in May and June, it becomes the center of the motorcycle world. Thousands of motorcycle lovers gather to watch and compete in motorcycle road racing's oldest event, the Isle of Man Tourist Trophy.

The first TT was held in 1907. It soon became the greatest event in motorcycle road racing. For nearly 70 years, no rider's career could be complete without a win at the TT. The island's fearsome road course is the ultimate test of a rider's skill and courage. Over the decades, dozens have lost their lives trying to tame the TT's twisting mountain roads.

The TT was part of the World Championship from 1949 to 1976. By the 1970s, the island's unforgiving course was judged too dangerous for modern bikes. The bikes were just too fast. The TT continues, however. It remains one of motorcycle road racing's most popular events.

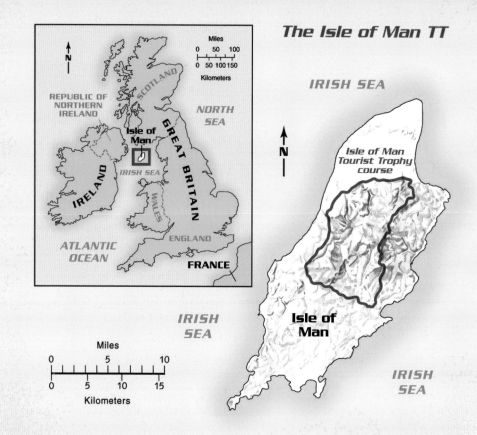

The Isle of Man TT

Geoff Duke, Isle of Man, 1951

Riders race down a straightaway during the 2007 Isle of Man

But the riders weren't the only ones competing. Motorcycle makers had long understood the value of racing. Winning races brought the companies fame, glory, and sales. So they went all out to build the best bikes possible.

Manufacturers also raced to learn. There's an old saying, "Racing improves the breed." Pushing bikes to the limit in competition was a great way to test new ideas.

The First World Championships

After World War II (1939–1945), the FICM changed its name to the Federation Internationale de Motorcyclisme (FIM, or International Federation of Motorcycling). In 1949 the FIM started the first world championship series. Riders earned points in the series' six events. GP races were held in Belgium, Switzerland, Italy, and Northern Ireland. The Isle of Man TT and the Dutch TT (in the Netherlands) were also included.

Riders competed for titles in several classes. The classes were based on the size of the bikes' engines, measured in cubic centimeters (cc). The lower three classes were for 350cc, 250cc, and 125cc. The top class was 500cc. Sometimes called the class of kings, the top class featured the biggest, most powerful bikes and Europe's best riders.

The sport kept growing in the 1950s. The competition was fierce. Great Britain and Italy produced the best riders and the best motorcycles. Italians Umberto Masetti and Libero Liberati won 500cc titles in the 1950s. Geoff Duke of Great Britain won six world titles in the first half of the decade. His total included four 500cc crowns and two 350cc titles.

The late 1950s belonged to another British rider—John Surtees. Surtees won four championships riding for the Italian MV Agusta factory team. A factory team is one that is directly supported by the motorcycle manufacturing company.

The top manufacturers spent lots of money trying to squeeze every bit of speed out of the bikes. They tried different engine designs. The idea was to produce the most power in the smallest, lightest package. All the 500cc engines of the time were four-stroke machines. But some had just one cylinder (fuel-burning compartment), while others had two, four, six, or even eight.

Geoff Duke hugs his bike as he roars down a hill at the 1955 Isle of Man TT. Riders crouch like this in order to glide through the air as easily as possible.

Streamlining

In the 1950s, manufacturers added fairings (covers) to the front and rear of the bikes. The fairings allowed the motorcycle to cut through the air smoothly. The results were record-breaking speeds. In fact, the bikes were too fast. For example, Moto Guzzi's 499cc V8 of 1957 had a top speed of 178 miles (286 km) per hour. That kind of speed was too dangerous for narrow, treelined road courses such as the Isle of Man. One slip could send a rider crashing to his death. In 1958 the FIM took a safety measure by setting limits on the size of the fairings used.

Right: John Surtees, 1956

Two-Stroke vs. Four-Stroke Engines

Road racing motorcycles are powered by internal combustion engines. These machines create power by burning a mixture of fuel (gasoline) and air. The mixture is burned inside the engine's cylinder or cylinders. (Over the years, racing motorcycle engines have had anywhere between one and eight cylinders). Early grand prix bikes had four-stroke engines *(left)*. Two-stroke engines *(next page)* took over in the 1970s. But in 2002, the FIM created the MotoGP class, featuring bikes with 990cc, four-stroke engines. In 2007 the rules were changed again. All MotoGP bikes have 800cc engines.

The Four-Stroke Engine

A four-stroke engine *(right)* burns a mixture of fuel and air. It uses a set of valves to allow fuel and exhaust into and out of the cylinder.

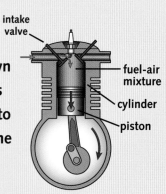

1. INTAKE STROKE
The piston moves down the cylinder and draws the fuel-air mixture into the cylinder through the intake valve.

intake valve, fuel-air mixture, cylinder, piston

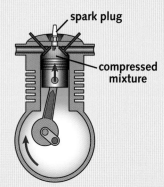

2. COMPRESSION STROKE
The piston moves up and compresses the fuel-air mixture. The spark plug ignites the mixture, creating combustion (burning).

spark plug, compressed mixture

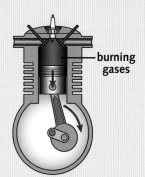

3. POWER STROKE
The burning gases created by combustion push the piston downward. This gives the engine its power.

burning gases

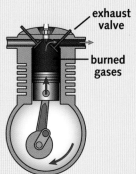

4. EXHAUST STROKE
The piston moves up again and pushes out the burned-out exhaust gases through the exhaust valve.

exhaust valve, burned gases

1. INTAKE/EXHAUST STROKE

The piston moves downward, uncovering the exhaust port and cylinder intake. The exhaust (burned gases from the previous combustion) escapes through the exhaust port. The mixture of air, gas, and oil enters the engine's crankcase. (The oil in the mixture keeps the piston and crankshaft lubricated.)

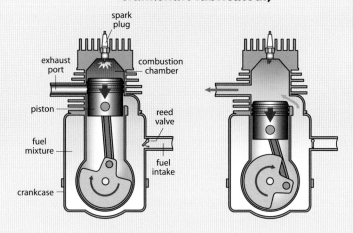

2. COMPRESSION/POWER STROKE

As the piston moves back up, it compresses the fuel, oil, and air mixture. At the same time, the remaining exhaust is pushed out of the exhasut port. The spark plug ignites the compressed mixture, creating combustion (burning).

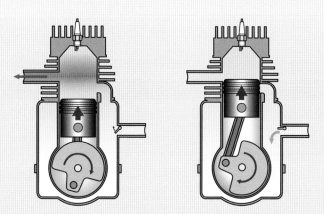

The Two-Stroke Engine

A two-stroke engine *(below)* burns a mixture of fuel, air, and oil. Unlike a four-stroke, its simple design does not use valves to control the flow of fuel and exhaust. Two-stroke engines create more power than four-stroke engines but are much less fuel-efficient. And since two-stroke engines burn oil as well as gas, they create more air pollution than four-stroke engines.

Right: Mike Hailwood leans his 500cc MV Agusta into a turn during a 1965 race at Brands Hatch in Kent, England. *Below:* Hailwood, this time on a 250cc Honda, prepares for a 1967 race at Brands Hatch.

The 1960s:
The MV Agusta Years

MV Agusta ruled the 1960s. The thundering red and silver bikes won every 500cc title in the decade. The team also won many titles in the smaller classes.

The best riders of the day wanted to ride for MV Agusta. And in the early 1960s, the best rider in the world was Mike Hailwood. In 1962, the 22-year-old Brit became the youngest 500cc world champion. Three more titles followed in the next three years.

Like many other riders of the time, "Mike the Bike" Hailwood didn't just race in the top class. Over a race weekend, he often raced in four different classes on four different bikes. In the smaller classes, Hailwood raced for Honda, a new Japanese factory team. Honda was the first Japanese company to enter European racing. Other Japanese companies, including Yamaha and Suzuki, would soon follow.

In 1966 Italian Giacomo Agostini became MV Agusta's top rider. For the next seven years, King Ago and MV Agusta were unbeatable, winning seven straight 500cc titles. (They also won seven straight 350cc titles, beginning in

14

Gary Hocking

In 1961 Gary Hocking *(right)* of Rhodesia (present-day Zimbabwe) rode MV Agusta to both the 350cc and 500cc titles. A brilliant talent, Hocking might have won more titles. But he was horrified by the dangers of the sport. In June 1962, one of his friends was killed while racing at the Isle of Man TT. Grief-stricken, Hocking quit motorcycle racing. But like so many racers, he still craved speed. So he tried racing Formula One cars. Six months later, the 25-year-old was killed in a crash during practice.

1968.) In fact, MV and Agostini were too good. Agostini often won races by minutes instead of seconds. Without much competition, the racing became stale.

The 1970s:
The Two-Stroke Revolution

In the early 1970s, Yamaha and Suzuki tried a different kind of 500cc engine. Two-stroke engines had been used for years in the smaller classes. But no one had made a two-stroke for the big 500cc class. Yamaha and Suzuki believed that these smaller, lighter engines were the key to beating MV Agusta.

The Yamaha two-stroke won a few races in 1973. Then, in 1974, Agostini joined the team. The following year, he became the first rider to win a 500cc world championship on a

Giacomo Agostini roars up a hill during the 1967 Isle of Man TT. King Ago's record of 15 world championships will probably never be broken.

The ultrafocused Kenny Roberts leans his 500cc Yamaha low on his way to his third straight world championship in 1980.

two-stroke. Within a few years, every 500cc GP bike was a two-stroke.

The 1976 and 1977 seasons were ruled by Barry Sheene and his two-stroke Suzuki. Handsome, fun-loving, and fast, Sheene became a superstar. He was a household name in Europe.

But Sheene's time on top did not last. In 1978 Yamaha introduced a hot young American rider to the GP scene. His name was Kenny Roberts, and he would turn the GP racing world upside down. Roberts brought a whole new riding

style to GP racing. The cocky Californian had developed his skills on the slippery dirt tracks of his home state. Even on pavement, Roberts slid in and out of turns like he was on skis. He used his entire body to control the bike. While European riders just leaned their backs and shoulders into turns, Roberts hung off the side of his bike. He leaned the bike so far over that he nearly touched the road. His style allowed him to turn at higher speeds and hit the straights with more momentum.

Grand National: Motorcycle Racing, American Style

Over the years, American motorcycle racing never enjoyed the same popularity as GP racing in Europe. As a result, U.S. Grand National racing tended to be very laidback. Riders didn't earn much money. They were in it for the thrills. With its many dirt track races, the Grand National series of the 1960s and 1970s was a low-down, dirty, rough-and-tumble sport. Riders slid through turns at full throttle. With one foot scraping the ground, they swung their back wheels sideways, kicking up showers of dirt behind them. The competition wasn't polite, either. If one rider knocked another rider over, he could count on having the favor returned before too long. Postrace fistfights weren't unusual. It was all part of the fun, and the fans loved it.

In 1976 the AMA restructured its racing events. It split the Grand Nationals, creating a series just for road racing, the AMA Superbike Championship. Dirt track racing continued, but it was never quite the same. Grand Nationals fans still look on the 1960s and 1970s as the good old days of U.S. motorcycle racing.

Left: Kenny Roberts (80) "torpedoes" John Hately (43) during a 1971 race, knocking down both riders. This kind of wheel-to-wheel, elbow-to-elbow action made Grand National racing a thrill to watch. *Right:* Kenny Roberts gets his Yamaha sideways during a Grand National flat track race.

Freddie Spencer *(center, in blue and white)* celebrates his victory at the 1985 Spanish 500cc Motorcycle Grand Prix. Eddie Lawson *(left, in red)* came in second.

The European riders couldn't keep up with Roberts and his yellow and black Yamaha. King Kenny won the 500cc titles in 1978, 1979, and 1980.

The 1980s:
The American Invasion

Roberts's success opened the door for American riders in GP racing. They would go on to dominate the class of kings, winning seven out of ten 500cc titles in the 1980s.

And the Americans were winning on Japanese bikes. By the 1980s, Honda, Yamaha, and Suzuki were miles ahead of the pack. The Japanese builders were investing millions of dollars in their racing programs. Their bikes were by far the best in the field. They would go on to dominate the 500cc class for the rest of the century.

Twenty-one-year-old Freddie Spencer, another American, won the GP title in his first season in 1983. He remains the youngest world champion. Two years later, Fast Freddie did "the double." He rode Hondas to championships in both the 500cc and 250cc classes.

Another American, Eddie Lawson, soon emerged. Steady Eddie brought a mix of speed and smarts to the sport. He knew that championships were the goal. Winning races earned the most points. But crashing out of a race earned zero points. Lawson avoided taking risks just to score a win. He was happy with second-place finishes if he won the title at the end of the season. Steady Eddie's patient approach earned him titles for Yamaha in 1984, 1986, 1988, and 1989.

By the end of the decade, American riders and Japanese bikes had become an unbeatable combination. But their reign wasn't over yet. In fact, the best was yet to come.

The 1990s: Rainey, Schwantz, and Doohan

GP racing in the early 1990s can be summed up in three words: Rainey vs.

Schwantz. Californian Wayne Rainey was intense, focused, and obsessed with winning. Kevin Schwantz was a fun-loving Texan. Rainey rode for Yamaha, while Schwantz rode for Suzuki. In the early 1990s, they were the two best riders in the world. Their on-track battles made for the most exciting racing in the history of the 500cc class. The two Americans kept crowds on their feet throughout those years.

Sadly, their exciting rivalry ended in tragedy. In 1993 Rainey crashed at the Italian Grand Prix at Misano. He was left paralyzed from the chest down. His riding career was over.

Over the years, only one rider had been able to keep up with Schwantz and Rainey. However, injuries had kept Mick Doohan from becoming champion. In 1994 everything came together for the tough Australian. His Honda team had designed a bike with a powerful engine. Nicknamed the big bang (it was extremely loud), the engine could outrun everything else on the track. The

Above: In 1993 Wayne Rainey (1) and Kevin Schwantz (34) vied for first place in the Spanish Grand Prix. *Below:* Australian Mick Doohan does a victory lap with the Aussie flag after his victory in the 500cc British Motorcycle Grand Prix in 1997.

combination of Doohan and Honda was unbeatable. Beginning in 1994, the Australian rider romped to five straight titles. His best season came in 1997, when he won 12 out of 16 races.

The 2000s: Rossi and MotoGP

By the year 2000, two-stroke engine technology had reached its peak. The manufacturers had run out of ways to

Right: Valentino Rossi on board his Honda RC211V on his way to the MotoGP championship in 2002. In 2004 the familiar yellow #46 would move to Yamaha and win two more titles. **Below:** Rossi, wearing a T-shirt saying "how spectacular" in Italian, holds up his trophy after winning the Australian Grand Prix in 2004.

get more power and speed out of the engines. Simply put, racing was no longer improving the breed.

More important, two-stroke engines weren't even made for regular street bikes anymore. Two-strokes are very dirty and inefficient. They burn a mixture of fuel and oil, creating far more air pollution than four-strokes. Because of this, many governments had outlawed the use of two-strokes for everyday street bikes.

With these concerns in mind, the FIM announced a major change to the sport for 2002. The FIM dropped the 500cc class. In its place, it allowed four-stroke engines of up to 990cc. The new class was called MotoGP. (The 250cc and 125cc classes would remain the same.)

The change brought new life to the sport. Manufacturers had to test out new ideas. And the new technology would help to improve the breed. Still, the new class began the same way the old one ended—with Honda on top. But this time, the champion was a colorful young Italian named Valentino Rossi. Many people say Rossi is the best motorcycle racer ever. He is clever, brave, and rarely makes mistakes.

Rossi was the last rider to win a 500cc championship. He didn't miss a beat on the new bikes, winning the first MotoGP title in 2002. More titles followed. By 2005 Rossi had won five straight world championships. The Italian's string of titles was finally broken in 2006. Mechanical failures knocked him out of several races. This allowed American Nicky Hayden to claim the crown for Honda.

The 2007 season brought more changes. The 990cc bikes were just too fast. So the FIM changed the size limit of the engines to 800cc. And for the first time in 34 years, a non-Japanese company won the top-class title. Italian manufacturer Ducati ran away with the championship. Australian Casey Stoner rode his Ducati to 10 wins in 17 races. Ducati's performance reminded some of the MV Agusta days. The exciting sport of motorcycle road racing had come full circle.

Above: The "Kentucky Kid," Nicky Hayden of Owensboro, Kentucky, celebrates winning the 2006 MotoGP World Championship at the last race of the season in Valencia, Spain. *Left:* Casey Stoner and his Ducati were an unbeatable combination in 2007.

Chapter Two

MOTORCYCLE ROAD RACING CULTURE

Motorcycle road racing has grown tremendously since the FIM introduced that six-race championship in 1949. Over the years, more and more events have been added. As many as 18 races take place in a season (the number varies from year to year). The championship has spread across the world. Riders from Australia, South Africa, Brazil, and many other countries have competed. Races have been held on five continents. Countries such as Japan, Malaysia, China, Turkey, Qatar, Australia, South Africa, Brazil, and the United States host races. MotoGP has become one of the world's most popular sports, with hundreds of millions of fans in dozens of countries.

The race season begins in March and ends in October or November.

Riders earn points based on how they finish each race. The winner gets the most points, second place a few less, and so on. The rider with the most points at the end of the season is the world champion.

MotoGP: The Bikes

MotoGP bikes are expensive, high-tech machines. Teams spend tens of millions of dollars to build and develop their bikes.

MotoGP motorcycles use all the latest technology and materials. Many bike parts are made out of carbon fiber. Carbon fiber is strong but lightweight. (Weight is crucial. The lighter the bike is, the less work the engine has to do to get the bike moving.) Other parts, including the engine, are made with

Valentino Rossi's Yamaha M1 MotoGP bike is one of the most sophisticated racing vehicles ever built. Every year the teams build new bikes using the latest ideas and technology.

Fans in Valencia, Spain, line the hillsides of the track to watch their countryman Dani Pedrosa of the Honda factory team.

special alloys (mixed metals). The chassis and engine block are made of strong, lightweight aluminum alloy.

Engineers also focus on creating aerodynamic motorcycles. They use wind tunnels to try out different-shaped fairings and parts. The idea is to find a design that will cut through the air as smoothly as possible.

The Race Weekend

Most motorcycle road racing events take place from Friday through Sunday. The teams arrive a few days early. They set up shop and get ready for the weekend. For MotoGP events, Friday is practice day. Qualifying is held on Saturday. Sunday is race day.

On practice days, the track is open to the teams for two practice sessions. The sessions last 60 or 90 minutes. The riders test the bikes to learn how they run on the track. The goal of practice is to set up the bike for race day. The team can make many small changes to the motor-cycles. They adjust the bike's suspension

Rider Gear

Riders wear specially designed safety equipment. Helmets are a must, of course. Rider helmets are made of carbon fiber. They are practically indestructible. A rider's suit (called leathers) is made of kangaroo leather. Kangaroo hide is very thin and light. But it is also very strong. It doesn't rip easily. Elbow and shoulder pads cushion the impact from falls. Riders also wear a special back pad that was created by Barry Sheene. The pad allows the rider to bend forward but doesn't allow his back to bend backward.

(the parts that connect the wheels to the main part of the bike). The suspension's job is to keep the tires in contact with the road as much as possible. When the back tire isn't gripping the ground, it can't drive the bike forward. The engine's power is being wasted. When the front tire isn't gripping the ground, the bike doesn't turn as easily.

Most suspension changes are very small. But they can make all the difference on race day. For a bumpy track, the bike needs to have a soft setup. The suspension must be able to bounce up and down to keep the bike glued to the road. Smooth tracks allow the bikes to use a stiffer suspension. Teams figure out their setup during Friday practice.

Track Safety

Through the 1970s, motorcycle road racing was one of the world's deadliest sports. Riding a motorcycle at 200 miles (320 km) per hour will always be dangerous. But the sport has become much safer in the last 30 years. The biggest improvements have come by making the tracks safer. Road courses are rarely used in major events. (The Isle of Man TT lost its world championship status because of safety issues.) Instead, the racing takes place on tracks. All modern tracks have huge runoff areas. Drivers have plenty of room to slow down before hitting a wall or barrier. The runoffs are usually filled with gravel (nicknamed kitty litter). The thick gravel gives the riders a bit of cushion during falls. And it also slows down a sliding rider and his bike.

Qualifying

Saturday is qualifying day. This is when the competition truly starts. Riders qualify to decide their place on the starting grid of the race.

A qualifying session lasts about an hour. The riders run several laps, pushing their bikes to the limit. Their goal is to complete the fastest lap of the session. At the end of qualifying, the rider with the fastest lap wins pole position. This is the first spot on the starting grid on race day. The rider with the second-fastest qualifying lap gets to line up second on the grid, or P2. The rider with the third-best time lines up P3, and so on.

Qualifying position is a big key to

DID YOU KNOW?
MotoGP bikes can reach speeds of 210 miles (338 km) per hour in a straight line. They also have strong brakes. They can go from 200 miles (320 km) per hour to a dead stop in just a few seconds.

Nicky Hayden pops a wheelie on a qualifying lap. MotoGP bikes are so powerful that they can wheelie whether the rider wants them to or not.

Riders on the grid just seconds before the start of the 2006 Italian GP at Mugello. Sete Gibernau (15) is on pole, closest to the start/finish line. Loris Capirossi (65) is P2. Valentino Rossi (46) is P3. Nicky Hayden (69) is P4, first on the second row.

success on race day. Riders at the front of the grid have fewer bikes to pass for the lead. Bikes stuck at the back of the grid can get slowed down in traffic or caught up in crashes.

Race Day

Sunday is race day. It's the time to see which team's hard work will pay off. And it's the time to put on a thrilling show for the fans.

The racing begins in the early afternoon. In MotoGP, the fans get to watch three races. The show starts

with the 125cc race. Then the 250cc bikes take to the track. After the smaller classes are finished, it's time for the main event—MotoGP.

The riders line up on the starting grid. Just before the race begins, they do a warm-up lap. This gives them a chance to warm up their tires and engines. At the end of the lap, the riders take their spots on the grid. They crouch on their bikes and rev their engines to a high-pitched whine. MotoGP races feature standing starts. The riders and their bikes stand still

on the grid, ready for the start. When a set of lights in front of them turn off, the race has begun!

The crowd roars as the motorcycles scream down the track toward the first turn. Within seconds, the bikes are speeding at more than 150 miles (241 km) per hour. The riders are just inches apart, fighting for position. The first turn of the first lap is usually the most dangerous part of the race. As many as 20 bikes are packed together. Every rider fights for position. Sometimes there just isn't enough room for everybody. This is when crashes can happen.

Above: Led by Valentino Rossi (46, far left), the entire MotoGP field screams toward turn one at the start of the Turkish GP in Istanbul. *Left:* Casey Stoner (27) leads Nicky Hayden (1), Dani Pedrosa (26), and Valentino Rossi (46) early on during the 2007 Australian GP at Phillip Island.

As the race goes on, the riders spread out. The fastest bikes break away from the pack. The slower "backmarkers" battle for the lower positions.

MotoGP races are about 62 miles (100 km) long. Depending on the length of the track, this usually comes out to between 25 and 30 laps. The races last about 40 to 45 minutes. For the riders, every second is intense.

A rider uses his entire body to control the bike. He uses his legs, hips, and back muscles to lean the bike into turns. On the straights, he tucks his head and body behind the fairing. The rider wants to be as low as possible to allow the bike to glide smoothly through the air. Riders also use their hands and feet. They twist the throttle, which is part of the handlebar grip. They squeeze a lever on the handlebars to control the front-wheel brakes. They use a foot lever to control the rear-wheel brakes.

Learning to Fall

Crashing is part of racing. Even the best riders crash from time to time. The trick is to not get hurt in a crash. Riders learn the right way to fall off their bikes, which is to slide off the bike. Sliding allows the rider to "scrub off" speed, avoiding injuries. Riders rarely get hurt if they can slide off the bike.

The worst injuries come when a rider is thrown from the bike. The rider has no chance to control the fall. Instead of sliding, the rider can wind up rolling and tumbling, with brutal results. Broken arms, legs, ankles, feet, hands, fingers, wrists, and ribs can make a rider think twice about ever riding again.

The best riders make it all look easy. They have a knack for knowing just what the bike can do. And they also know what their opponents can do. For example, Valentino Rossi will hang back and study the rider ahead of him. He'll follow his opponent for a lap or two, looking for a weakness. If a rider is slower through a certain turn, Rossi will hang close as they come up to that turn. Then he will make his move and shoot past.

MotoGP races are famous for their thrilling finishes. It's not unusual for a rider to steal the lead on the last lap. Some races are won by a fraction of a second. But a rider who is holding a big lead will often give the crowd a show at the end. The most popular move is to do a wheelie across the finish line. Valentino Rossi sometimes stands up on his bike and bows to the crowd. It's all part of the fun and exciting atmosphere of motorcycle road racing.

Valentino Rossi applauds to the crowd after yet another win at the British GP at Donington Park in 2004.

MotoGP Tracks

MotoGP World Championship races have been held on every continent except Antarctica, although most of the races are held in Europe. Each track has its own unique shape and layout. These are the courses for the 2008 MotoGP season.

Grand Prix of Qatar

Losail Circuit
Doha, Qatar

3.3 miles (5.4 km)

Grand Prix of Spain

Jerez Circuit
Jerez, Spain

2.7 miles (4.4 km)

Grand Prix of Portugal

Estoril Circuit
Estoril, Portugal

2.6 miles (4.2 km)

Grand Prix of China

Shanghai International Circuit
Shanghai, China

3.4 miles (5.5 km)

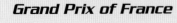

Grand Prix of France

Le Mans Bugatti GP Circuit
Le Mans, France

2.7 miles (4.4 km)

NORTH AMERICA

Monterey, California

Speedway, Indiana

SOUTH AMERICA

Europe's MotoGP Tracks

Donington, England

Assen, the Netherlands

Chemnitz, Germany

Brno, Czech Republic

Le Mans, France

Barcelona, Spain

Mugello, Italy

Rimini, Italy

Valencia, Spain

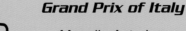

Grand Prix of Italy

Mugello Autodromo
Internazionale
Mugello, Italy
3.2 miles (5.2 km)

Grand Prix of Catalunya

Circuit de Catalunya
Barcelona, Spain

2.8 miles (4.6 km)

Grand Prix of Valencia

Circuit de la
Comunitat Valenciana
Valencia, Spain
2.5 miles (4.0 km)

Grand Prix of Malaysia

Sepang
International Circuit
Kuala Lumpur, Malaysia
3.4 miles (5.5 km)

Grand Prix of Australia

Phillip Island Circuit
Phillip Island, Australia

2.7 miles (4.4 km)

Grand Prix of Japan

Twin Ring Motegi
Motegi, Japan

3.0 miles (4.8 km)

Grand Prix of Indianapolis

Indianapolis Motor Speedway
Speedway, Indiana

2.6 miles (4.2 km)

Grand Prix of San Marino

Misano World Circuit
Rimini, Italy

2.6 miles (4.2 km)

Grand Prix of the Czech Republic

Automotodrom Brno
Brno, Czech Republic
3.3 miles (5.4 km)

Grand Prix of the United States

Laguna Seca Raceway
Monterey, California
2.2 miles (3.6 km)

area of
inset
(facing page)

ASIA

EUROPE

Jerez,
Spain

Estoril,
Portugal

Valencia,
Spain

Shanghai,
China

Motegi,
Japan

AFRICA

Doha,
Qatar

Kuala Lumpur,
Malaysia

AUSTRALIA

Phillip Island, Australia

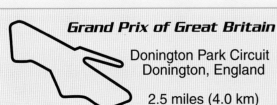

Grand Prix of Great Britain

Donington Park Circuit
Donington, England

2.5 miles (4.0 km)

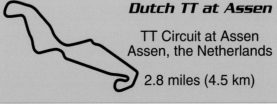

Dutch TT at Assen

TT Circuit at Assen
Assen, the Netherlands

2.8 miles (4.5 km)

Grand Prix of Germany

Sachsenring
Chemnitz, Germany

2.3 miles (3.7 km)

Giacomo Agostini (born 1942)

King Ago is the most successful motorcycle road racer of all time. Riding the world-beating MV Agusta bike, he destroyed all competition in the late 1960s and early 1970s. A graceful rider with movie-star looks, he remains a hero to Italian motorcycle racing fans.

Nationality: Italian

Seasons: 1964–1977

500cc Grand Prix wins: 68

World Championships: 15
8 500cc (1966–1972, 1975)
and 7 350cc (1968–1974)

Mick Doohan (born 1965)

The intense Australian overcame a string of injuries to win five world titles in a row. In the late 1990s, the Honda rider was far and away the best in the 500cc class. Tough and gritty, he was a fierce rider who intimidated his opponents.

Nationality: Australian

Seasons: 1988–1999

500cc Grand Prix wins: 54

World Championships: 5 (1994–1998)

Giacomo Agostini,
Isle of Man TT, 1967

Mick Doohan on his
500cc Honda, Spanish
Grand Prix, 1992

Geoff Duke (born 1923)

Geoff Duke was the first rider to win multiple world championships. He was also the first to win three titles in a row. The gentlemanly Brit owned the Isle of Man TT in the early 1950s, winning the event six times. Like John Surtees and Mike Hailwood, Duke tried his hand at Formula One racing but with little success.

Nationality: English

Seasons: 1948–1959

500cc Grand Prix wins: 22

World Championships: 6

4 500cc (1951, 1953–1955) and

2 350cc (1951–1952)

Mike Hailwood (1940–1981)

Many people say Mike the Bike was the greatest motorcycle road racer of all time. He was famous for his ability to win on any kind of bike under any conditions. Loved for his sportsmanship and generosity, he was a hero with the British public. He was killed in a car accident in 1981.

Nationality: British

Seasons: 1959–1968

500cc Grand Prix wins: 37

World Championships: 9

4 500cc (1962–1965), 2 350cc (1966–1967),

and 3 250cc (1961, 1966, 1967)

Geoff Duke,1960

Mike Hailwood rode a 250cc
Honda during his win in the
Isle of Man TT in 1967.

Eddie Lawson (born 1958)

Steady Eddie wasn't the most lovable rider in the world. He didn't care about being famous, and he didn't like to talk to the media. Instead, he let his riding speak for itself. After winning AMA Superbike titles in 1981 and 1982, he moved on to Europe to take on the world's best. His four world championships are tops among Americans.

Nationality: American

Seasons: 1983–1992

500cc Grand Prix wins: 31

World Championships: 4

  500cc (1984, 1986, 1988, 1989)

Wayne Rainey (born 1960)

The intense Californian ruled the 500cc class in the early 1990s. He was known for his coolness under pressure and his skill at setting up his bike. His battles with Kevin Schwantz made for some of the greatest motorcycle racing in history. But their rivalry ended with Rainey's terrible crash at Misano, Italy, in 1993. The accident left the three-time world champion paralyzed from the chest down. He later became the boss of the Yamaha factory team.

Nationality: American

Seasons: 1988–1993

500cc Grand Prix wins: 24

World Championships: 3

  500cc (1990–1992)

Eddie Lawson, French
Grand Prix, 1991

Wayne Rainey on
his 500cc Yamaha,
Spanish Grand Prix,
1993

Kenny Roberts (born 1951)

The cocky Californian changed motorcycle road racing forever. His wild, wheel-sliding style forced people to rethink what could be done on a motorcycle. And his success in Europe opened the door for many other great American riders. After retiring from racing, he went on to become a successful team owner. His son, Kenny Jr., won the 500cc World Championship in 2000.

Nationality: American

Seasons: 1978–1983

500cc Grand Prix wins: 22

World Championships: 3

500cc (1978–1980)

Valentino Rossi (born 1979)

The fun-loving Italian is one of the world's most famous athletes. He won the 500cc title in his second year in the class. Since then, few riders have been able to keep up with him. Mechanical problems have kept him from winning more titles in recent seasons, but no one doubts Rossi's talents.

Nationality: Italian

Seasons: 1996–

500cc/MotoGP wins: 62

World Championships: 7

1 500cc (2001), 4 MotoGP (2002–2005),

1 250cc (1999), and 1 125cc (1997)

Kenny Roberts on his
500cc Yamaha, 1980

Valentino Rossi and his 500cc
Yamaha during a race at
Laguna Seca, 2005

Kevin Schwantz (born 1964)

The tall, cocky Texan was the fastest rider of his time. His all-out riding style was a thrill to watch. But the Suzuki rider's wild approach often worked against him—he tended to crash a lot. Because of this, he often ended up secondbest behind his steadier rival, Wayne Rainey. After his racing career, Schwantz moved into the TV booth to do commentary for MotoGP broadcasts.

Nationality: American

Seasons: 1988–1995

500cc Grand Prix wins: 25

World Championships: 1 (1993)

Barry Sheene (1950–2003)

Sheene was motorcycle road racing's first true superstar. In the 1970s, he was a household name in Europe and one of Great Britain's biggest celebrities. Fans loved his charm, good looks, and toughness. His career was cut short by several brutal injuries. He died of cancer at the age of 53.

Nationality: British

Seasons: 1970–1984

500cc Grand Prix wins: 19

World Championships: 2
500cc (1976–1977)

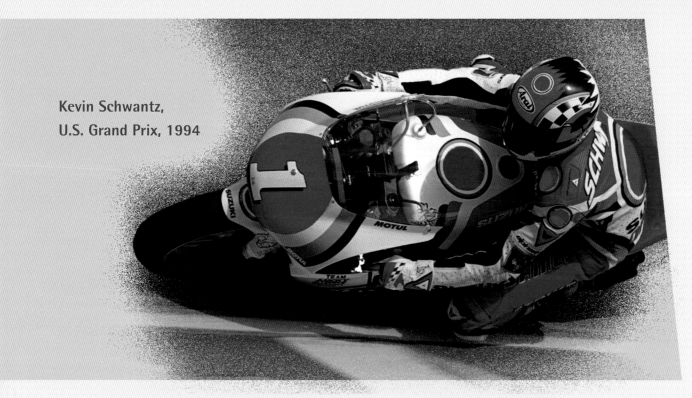

Kevin Schwantz,
U.S. Grand Prix, 1994

Barry Sheene on his
500cc Suzuki, Italian
Grand Prix, 1978

Freddie Spencer (born 1962)

The Shreveport, Louisiana, native enjoyed a brief but spectacular career. He burst on the 500cc scene in 1983. Just 21 years old at the time, he had the smarts and skills of a much older rider. He beat out Kenny Roberts in an exciting title fight to become the youngest 500cc world champion. In recent years, Spencer has worked as a TV commentator for AMA Superbike events.

Nationality: American
Seasons: 1980, 1982–1989, 1993
500cc Grand Prix wins: 20
World Championships: 3
  2 500cc (1983, 1985), 1 250cc (1985)

John Surtees (born 1934)

John Surtees owns a record that may never be matched. He is the only man to win a world championship on both two wheels and four wheels. He won four 500cc titles for MV Agusta in the late 1950s. Then he switched to Formula One, the world's top form of auto racing. He won the F1 world title for Ferrari in 1964.

Nationality: English
Seasons: 1953–1961
500cc Grand Prix wins: 22
World Championships: 7
  4 500cc (1956, 1958–1960), 3 350cc (1958–1960)

Freddie Spencer on his
250cc Honda, Spanish
Grand Prix, 1985

John Surtees, 1957

Glossary

aerodynamic: shaped so that air flows smoothly over and around an object

AMA: American Motorcyclist Association, a U.S.-based motorcycle organizing body

cc: cubic centimeters, the most common unit of measurement of the size of a motorcycle engine

chassis: the main frame of a motorcycle

FIM: Federation Internationale de Motorcyclisme, or International Federation of Motorcycling, a worldwide motorcycle organizing body based in Geneva, Switzerland

pole position: the first spot on the starting grid

prototypes: original, one-of-a-kind models

qualifying: the period during which riders compete to decide their position on the starting grid for the race; the rider with the fastest lap wins pole position

starting grid: the area where the riders line up before the start of the race. In most races, the order of the starting grid is decided by the speed of each rider's best qualifying lap.

superbike: a road-racing motorcycle that has been modified from a stock production bike

suspension: the set of parts that connect the wheels to the bike's chassis

throttle: the part of a motorcycle that controls the flow of fuel to the engine

Selected Bibliography

Duckworth, Mick. *Classic Racing Motorcycles*. Saint Paul: Motorbooks International, 2003.

Oxley, Mat. *Mick Doohan: Thunder from Down Under*. 2nd ed. Newbury Park, CA: Haynes North America, 2000.

Petrier, Marc. *FIM 1904–2004: 100 Years of Motorcycling*. Mies, Switzerland: Federation Internationale de Motocyclisme, 2004.

Scalzo, Joe. *Grand National: America's Golden Age of Motorcycle Racing*. Saint Paul: Motorbooks International, 2004.

Scott, Michael. *The 500cc World Champions: The Story of the Class of Kings*. Newbury Park, CA: Haynes North America, 2002.

Spalding, Neil. *MotoGP Technology*. Phoenix: David Bull Publishing, 2007.

Raby, Philip. *Motorbikes*. Minneapolis: Lerner Publications Company, 1999.

Smedman, Lisa. *From Boneshakers to Choppers: The Rip-Roaring History of Motorcycles*. Toronto: Annick Press, 2007.

Further Reading

Dubowski, Mark. *Superfast Motorcycles*. New York: Bearport Publishing, 2005.

Gifford, Clive. *Racing: The Ultimate Motorsports Encyclopedia*. Boston: Kingfisher, 2006.

Websites

Honda Racing Corporation History
http://world.honda.com/HRC/history/25thannivesary/index.html
Learn about Honda's rich racing history at the official website of the Honda Racing Corporation.

Nicky Hayden's Official Website
http://nickyhayden.com
Visit the official website of the Kentucky Kid, 2006 MotoGP World Champion Nicky Hayden, to get the latest news, view photos, and watch videos of Nicky's life and career.

The Official MotoGP Website
http://www.motogp.com
The official MotoGP website features the latest news and information about the most popular motorcycle road racing series on the planet.

Index

125 cc class, 10, 20, 28

250 cc class, 10, 14, 18, 20, 28

350 cc class, 10, 14, 15

500 cc class, 10, 11, 14, 15, 16, 18, 19, 20, 21

800 cc class, 12, 21

990 cc class, 12, 20, 21

Agostini, Giacomo, 14–16, 34–35

American Motorcycle Association (AMA), 7–8, 17

American Motorcycle Association Grand National, 8, 16, 17

American Motorcycle Association Superbike Championship, 17, 38, 44

Australian Grand Prix, 20, 29

AVUS (Automobil Verkehrs und Übungs Strasse), 8

British Grand Prix, 19

Capirossi, Loris, 28

Doohan, Mick, 19, 34

Ducati, 21

Duke, Geoff, 9, 11, 36

Dutch Tourist Trophy, 8, 10

fairings, 11

Federation Internationale de Motorcyclisme (FIM), 10, 11, 12, 20, 21, 22

Federation of American Motorcyclists (FAM), 7

Federation of International Motorcycle Clubs (FICM), 7, 10

Formula One, 15, 36, 44

four-stroke engine, 11, 12, 20

Gibernau, Sete, 28

Graham, Les, 10

Hailwood, Mike, 14, 36

Hayden, Nicky, 21, 27, 28, 29

Hildebrand and Wolfmuller, 6

Hocking, Gary, 15

Honda, 14, 18, 19, 20, 21, 24, 34

Isle of Man Tourist Trophy, 7, 8, 9, 10, 11, 15, 26, 36

Italian Grand Prix, 19, 28

Lawson, Eddie, 18, 38

MotoGP, 22, 42; class, 12, 20, 21; bike design, 23–25; bike speed, 4, 27; equipment, 25; event schedule, 24–25, 27–30; riders, 30

MotoGP World Championship, 4, 9, 21, 32–33

Moto Guzzi, 11

MV Agusta, 14, 15, 21, 34, 44

Pedrosa, Dani, 24, 29

Rainey, Wayne, 18–19, 38, 42

Roberts, Kenny, 16, 18, 40, 44

Rossi, Valentino, 20–21, 23, 28, 29, 31, 40

Schwantz, Kevin, 18–19, 38, 42

Sheene, Barry, 16, 25, 42

Spanish Grand Prix, 5, 18, 19

Spencer, Freddie, 18, 44

Stoner, Casey, 21, 29

Surtees, John, 11, 36, 44

Suzuki, 14, 15, 16, 18, 19, 42

Tourist Trophies (TTs), 8. See also: Dutch Tourist Trophy; Isle of Man Tourist Trophy

Turkish Grand Prix, 29

two-stroke engine, 12, 13, 15, 16, 19–20

Yamaha, 15, 16, 18, 19, 20, 23, 38

About the Author

Jeffrey Zuehlke is an author, editor, and motorsports enthusiast, who has published more than two dozen books for children. He lives in Saint Paul, Minnesota.

About the Consultant

Jeffrey San George is an engineer, technical consultant and lifetime motorcycle enthusiast with over 25 years of racing, adventure touring and mechanic experience. He lives in Franklin, Tennessee.

Photo Acknowledgments

The images in this book are used with the permission of: © Francisco Leong/AFP/Getty Images, pp. 4-5; © Fox Photos/Hulton Archive/Getty Images, pp. 6 (background), 9 (left); © SSPL/The Image Works, p. 6; © Topical Press Agency/Hulton Archive/Getty Images, pp. 7, 15 (left); © akg-images, p. 8; © Gary Calton/eyevine/ZUMA Press, p. 9 (right); © Central Press/Hulton Archive/Getty Images, p. 11 (top); © Terry Fincher/Keystone/Getty Images, p. 11 (bottom); © Gold & Goose, pp. 12, 13; © Ronald Dumont/Hulton Archive/Getty Images, p. 14 (left); © Express Newspapers/Hulton Archive/Getty Images, p. 14 (right); © Getty Images, p. 15 (right); © Steve Powell/Allsport/Getty Images, pp. 16, 41 (top); © Dan Mahony, p. 17 (both); © Richard Francis/Action Plus/Icon SMI, pp. 18, 44 (top), 45 (top); © Patrick Behar/TempSport/CORBIS, pp. 19 (top), 39 (both); AP Photo/Martin Cleaver, pp. 19 (bottom), 27; AP Photo/Franck Prevel, p. 20 (top); © Ryan Pierse/Getty Images, p. 20 (bottom); © Kazuhiro Nogi/AFP/Getty Images, p. 21 (left); © Denis Doyle/Getty Images, p. 21 (right); AP Photo/Rob Griffith, pp. 22- 23 (background); © ZSPORT/ZUMA Press, p. 23; AP Photo/Armado Franca, p. 24; AP Photo/Bas Czerwinski, p. 25; © Icon SMI, pp. 26, 28; REUTERS/Stringer Turkey, p. 29 (top); © Quinn Rooney/Getty Images, p. 29 (bottom); © Andrew Northcott/Getty Images, p. 30; AP Photo/Alastair Grant, p. 31; © Sutton Motorsports/ZUMA Press, p. 34 (top); © Mike Cooper/ALLSPORT/Getty Images, pp. 34 (bottom), 43 (top); © Bentley Archive/Popperfoto/Getty Images, p. 35 (top); © Chris Cole/Allsport/Getty Images, p. 35 (bottom); © Allsport/Hulton Archive/Getty Images, p. 36 (top); © Popperfoto/Getty Images, p. 36 (bottom); © Keystone Pictures/ZUMA Press, p. 37 (top); © Manchester Daily Express/SSPL/The Image Works, pp. 37 (bottom), 45 (bottom); © Eric Renard/TempSport/CORBIS, p. 38 (top); © Allsport UK/Getty Images, pp. 38 (bottom), 42 (bottom), 43 (bottom); © Jean-Yves Ruszniewski/TempSport/CORBIS, p. 40 (top); © Alterphotos/Panoramic/ZUMA Press, p. 40 (bottom); © Donald Miralle/Getty Images, p. 41 (bottom); © Shaun Botterill/Allsport/Getty Images, p. 42 (top); © Alan Webb/Getty Images, p. 44 (bottom). Ilustrations by © Laura Westlund/Independent Picture Service. Cover: © Holm Roehner/Bongarts/Getty Images.

DATE DUE			

Stamford Community Library

986 Main Road

Stamford, VT 05352

802-694-1379